ALICE IN LOVE

Poetry in Wonderland

Alice in Love
Poetry in Wonderland

VIVIENNE SAINT LOUIS

Copyright

All Rights Reserved. No part of this work may be transmitted, stored in an information retrieval system, or reproduced in anyway, electronically, graphically or mechanically, that include photocopying without prior written permission from the author. The only exception is by a reviewer who may quote short excerpts in the purposes of a review.

This is a work of fiction. Name, characters, places, incidents are either from the original source material Lewis Carroll's Alice in Wonderland or a product of the author's imagination. If real, it is used factiously. Any resemblance to actual person, living or dead, events or locales is entirely coincidental. The actions taken by the characters in this book should be relied upon to be exact of replicated as they may result in injury.

Alice in Wonderland by Lewis Carroll Published in 1865

This edition of Alice in Love: Poetry in Wonderland Published in 2020

ISBN 9798573833330

Imprint: Independently Published

Printed in the United States of America

Dedication

I dedicate this book to the seven amazing men who inspired it, the members of VICTON; Han Seungwoo, Kang Seungsik, Heo Chan, Lim Sejun, Do Hanse, Choi Byungchan, and Jung Subin. Through their incredible perseverance, their bond, and the love they have for their fans, they have inspired me not give up on my dreams no matter how for out of reach they seem. I watched them grow into the artist they are today, breaking records, winning awards, and shining through adversity after being ignored for years. They taught me by example that my own dreams are not unachievable even though they often seem that way. They taught me that I can succeed if I keep working hard towards my goals and never lose sight of them. These seven princes are my rock, and I am their Alice.

Thank you.

Preface

I started writing poems about love before I myself had ever really understood it. Even now, I find the emotion a mystery. As a science enthusiast, I know it is a series of chemicals in the brain like norepinephrine that cause people to feel euphoric and giddy. I know myself to have experience these feelings but much about love is still a mystery to me.

"Alice In Love – Poetry in Wonderland" illustrates all of the feelings I have associated with love in many of its forms, long lasting love, erotic love, playful love, obsessive love, self-love, selfless love, and affectionate love. But I leave which ones express each of these up to you the reader, to interpret.

To me love is like a wonderland. There is so much to experience and feel. There is euphoria, giddiness, a sense of losing oneself and even a sense of complete bewilderment. And with Alice's curious mind, I could weave through all of these in fantastical way that really brings it to life just how amazing the feeling of love is.

Happy Reading

V.V.

Down the Rabbit Hole

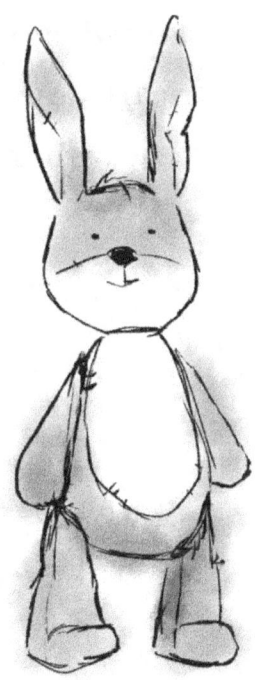

LOVE AND OTHER IMPOSSIBILITIES

Can I allow myself to believe it exist?
When til this day I have never been kissed?
Can I allow myself to dream of a crush?
When my knowledge is so rough?
When will my heart stop thumping when I am near them?

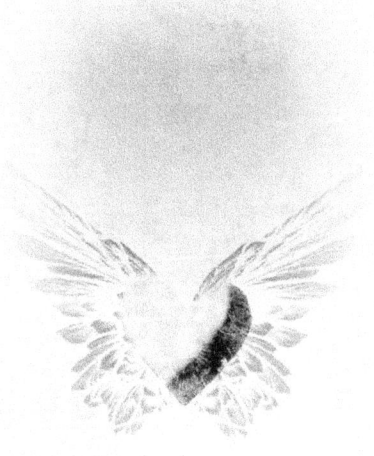

Why does my mouth get dry when I see them?
Can I give into this feeling?
When it is so foreign to me?
I dream of arms around me.

I imagine them squeezing me lovingly.
But can I allow myself to fantasize freely,
When the real thing still eludes me?
Will the real thing ever live up to my fantasies?
Or will I be crushed by the weight of them?

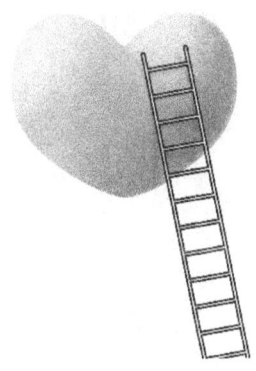

When You Look At Me Like That

When you look at me like that
I forget myself
I forget how to breathe
I forget not to give myself away
I forget my name
But you remember I like the way you look
at me
All my thoughts just fade away

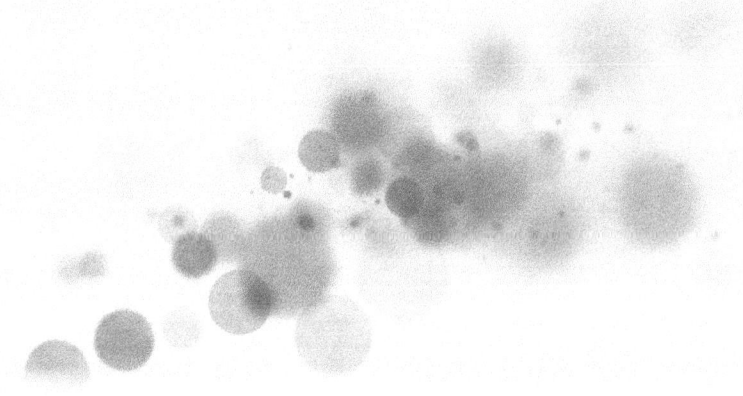

LITTLE JOYS

Your smile
Something sweet
Your arms around me.
A piece of music
Your love

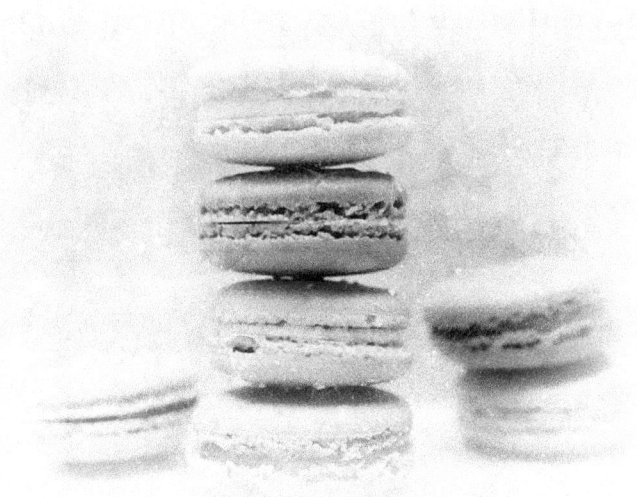

FLUTTER

Do not look at me like that.
Do not smile at me like the world would if you looked away.
I am too weak not to turn and blush cause you are too dazzling..
Do not touch me like that.
Do not squeeze my hand like you would fall apart if you let go cause I'd just might let you hold it forever.

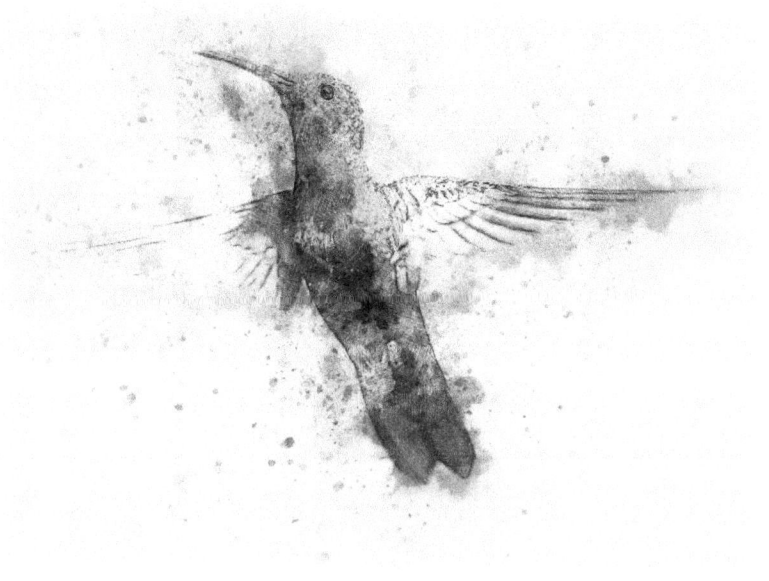

What is Love?

Is love unconditional?
Is love possible?
Is love magical?
Is love powerful?
Cause it is beautiful to me.
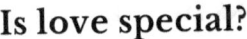
Cause it is painful to be alone.
Is love special?
Is love whimsical?
Is love joyful?
Because it is unreachable to me.
Is love spiritual?
Cause it is unbelievable to me.

The Mad Tea Party

I walk down a winding path
Stumble through trees
Creak over branches
Leap over puddles
And peer through a bush
To see something extraordinary

A white rabbit serving tea.
And a man in a hat as tall as he
Mismatched chairs before
Cups topped as high as me

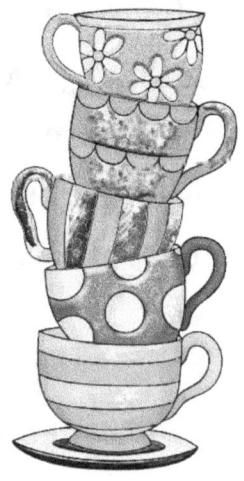

Sweets of all varieties
Balloons, tarts, and buzzing bees

You reach out your hand to me
I grasp it and walk timidly

You congratulate me
But it is not my birthday
You grin at me
And I cannot help but fill with glee

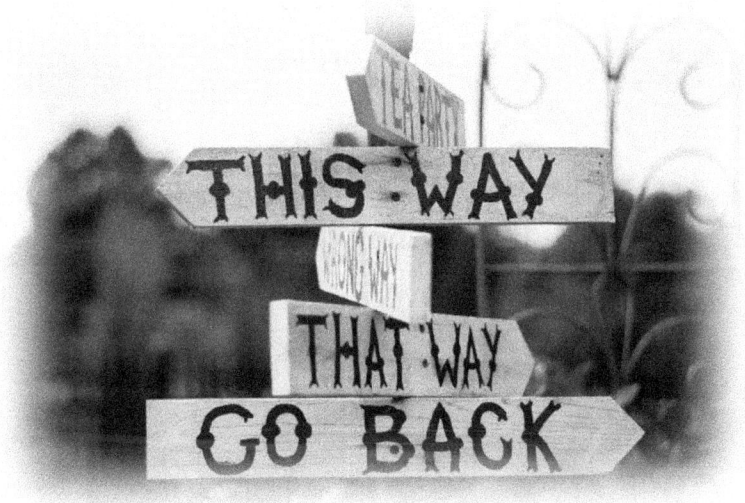

You serve me tea
It is as sweet as can be
You sing and clap as loud as can be
Nothing is as it should be
But I am loving this mad tea.

How Long Is Forever?

A minute
A day
A lifetime?
Can I stay here
In this place
Forever?

It is so strange this place
I do not know which way is up
It is so wild this journey
I do not know if I want it to end

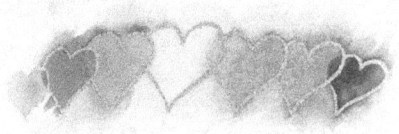

How long is forever?
Can you see it?
Can you touch it
Can it be measured?
Can I stay in your embrace forever?

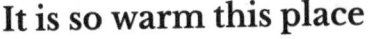

It is so warm this place
I do not want to be cold
again
It is so
wonderful
this place
I do not
want to leave
you ever

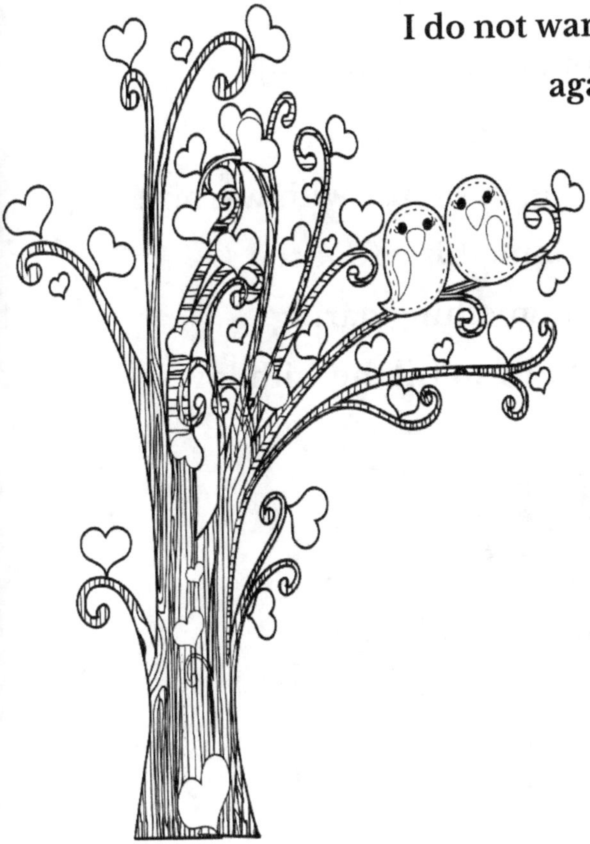

My Guilty Pleasure

Something yummy
Something fun
Something to fill me with warmth
Something foolish
Something daring
Something to fill me with love

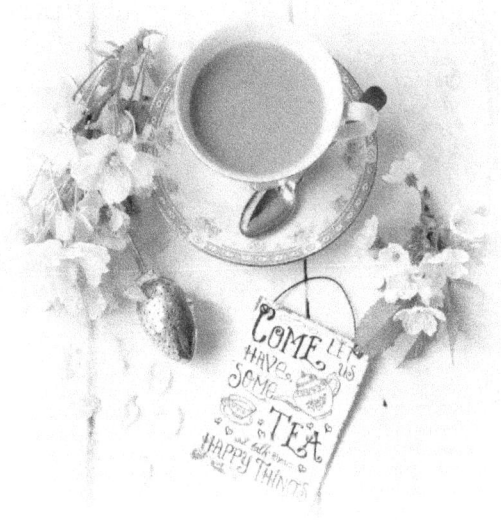

Welcome to Wonderland

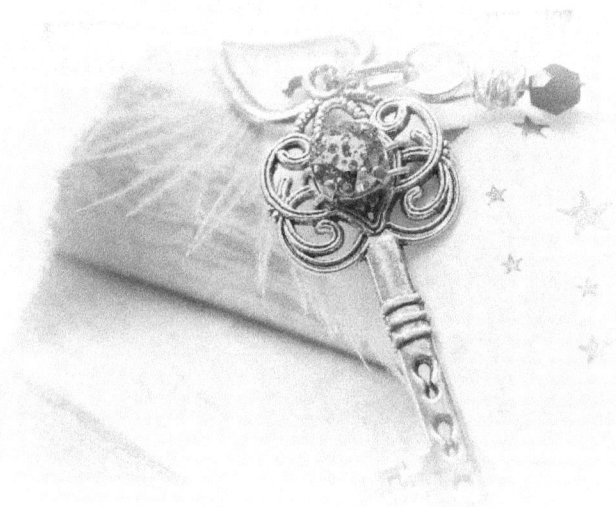

A forest of fantasy
You run ahead of me
I chase after you
A howling in the distance
A cry of Mayday
Is this a nightmare?
Then I see the light
Into the light I go
To you I follow
To you I sacrifice
The time of sorrow has ended

No more farewells
I embrace you
Petals fall around us
And I embrace my new world

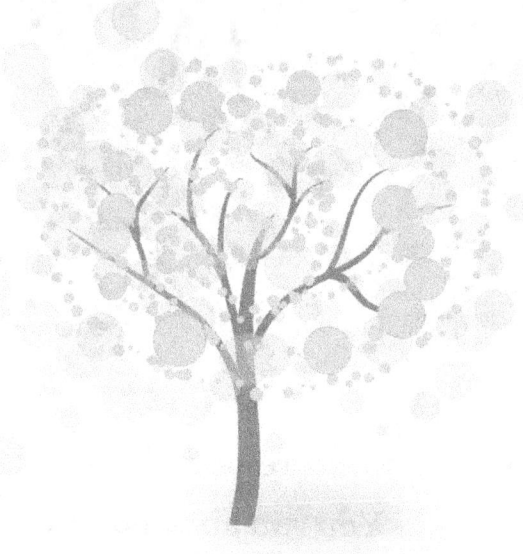

What Makes Me Blush

A kind word
A lingering stare
A heartbeat
A touch of my hair
A rare smile
A touch of your hand
A whisper
A pull of a strand

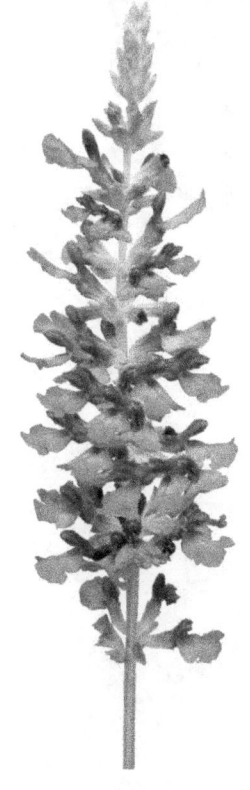

Before You

**Before you I was surviving
Now I am living**

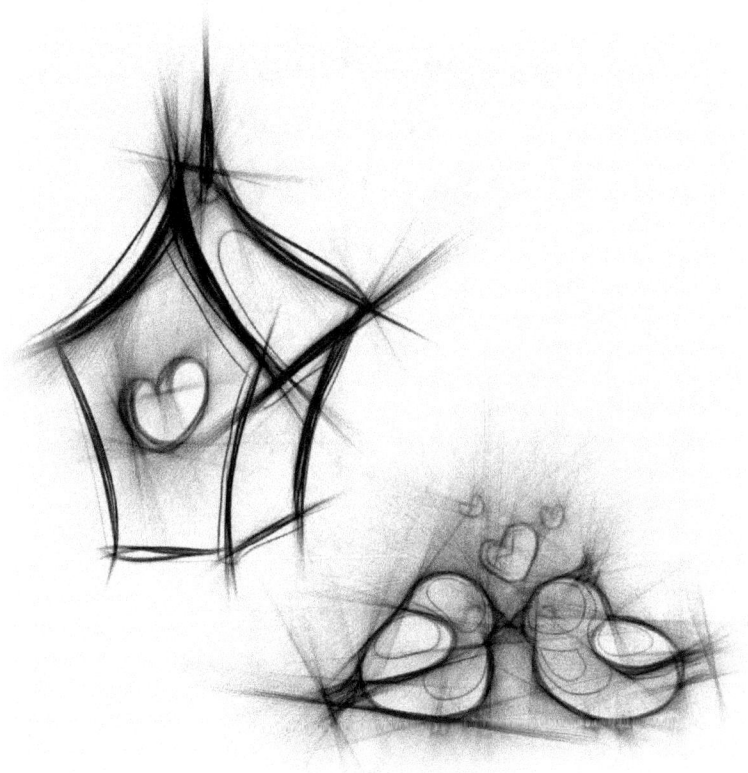

Everything's Sweeter Because It's With You

Eating
Walking
Dancing
Talking
Without you, life is bleak
Without you, I feel weak.

Mood

Your voice is my mood changer
No matter when I am feeling,
The sound of it both calm and excites me.

Look at me

Look at me
Look only at me
Kiss me
Kiss only me
Love me
Love only me
Forever

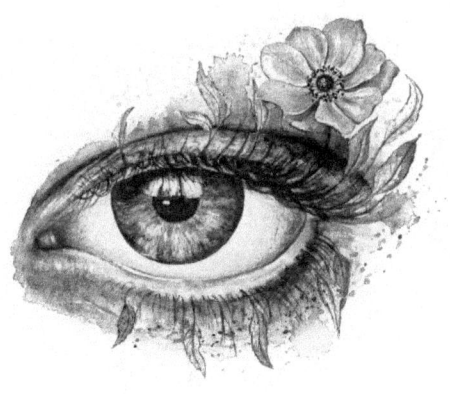

To My Angel

Know that your voice gives me strength
And I can listen to it a length
Know that your dreams are my dreams
And my love is as strong as it seems

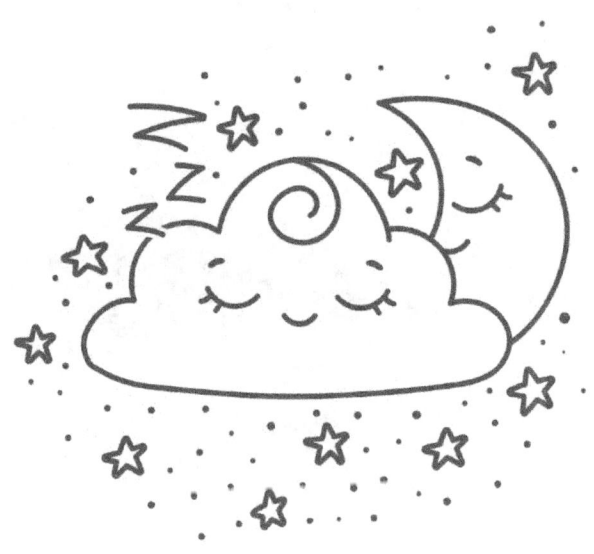

Trapped

I am trapped
In a cycle of loving you
And I never want it to end.

Drink me

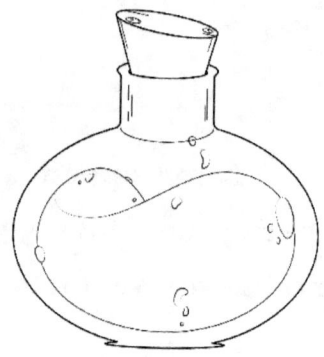

LOVE LIKE THAT

I want to love like that
The kind of love that changes you
The kind of love that never leaves you
It only keeps growing until the words do not
have to be said anymore
You just know.

I want to   love like
that.

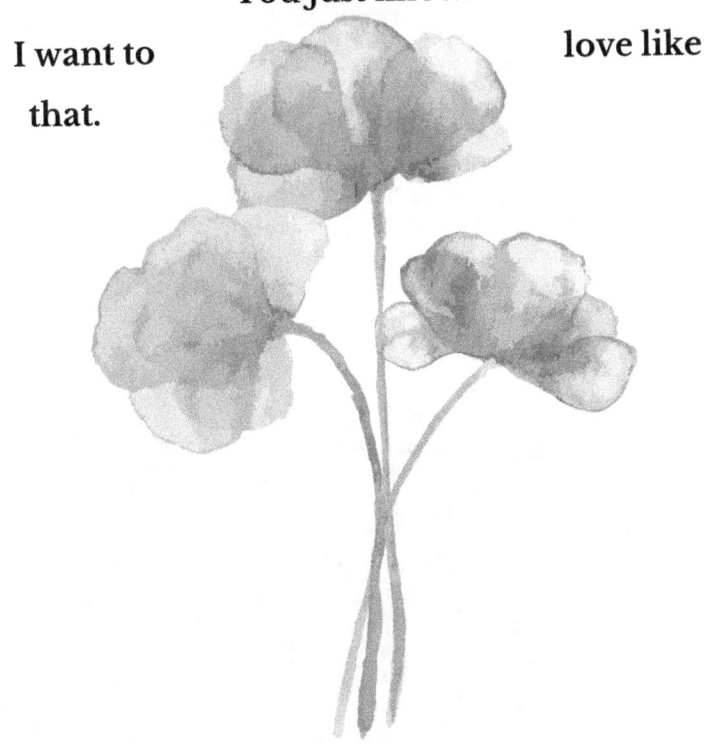

Lips

Your lips do something to me
Parting pouting smiling
Laughing panting smirking
They trigger my memories
Memories that make me think
Memories that make me weak

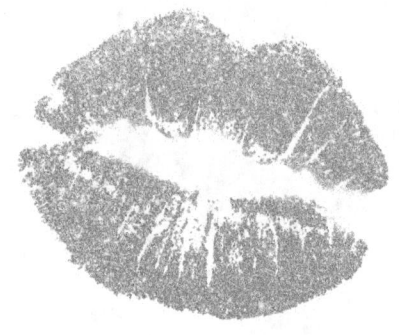

Kiss Me

Kiss me softly
Kiss me gently
Kiss me like you are saying goodbye
Kiss me like you are saving my life.

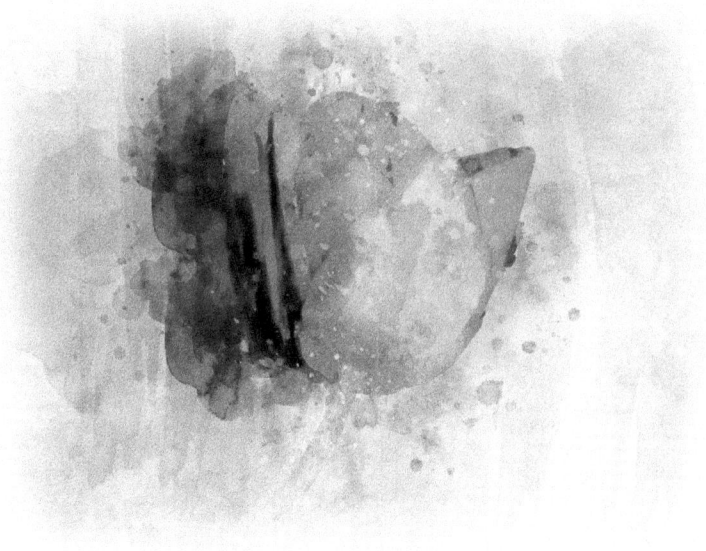

DOTING

You make me to shower you with affection
Buy you sweets
Give you warm hugs
And even sweeter kisses

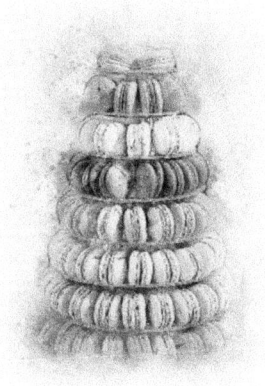

You make me want to show you off.
I want the world to know I love you.

You make me feel things.
Good things and warm fuzzy things
I laugh when you laugh
I cry when you cry
I hurt when someone hurts you

You make me stand up for you,
Even when you do not ask,
Even when you tell me not to.

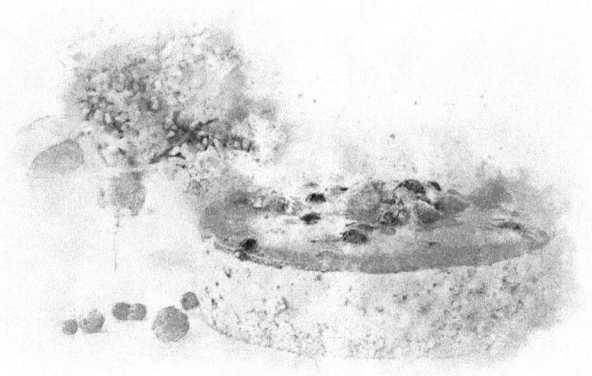

How I know I like you

A kind word
A lingering look
A heartbeat
A caress of my cheek
A brush of your lips.
A whisper in my ear.

Heartbeat

Do you hear my heart?
What does it sound like?
A bird beating its wings?
A cat purring?
A violinist plucking strings?
Is it louder when I am near you?
Does it stop when I kiss you?

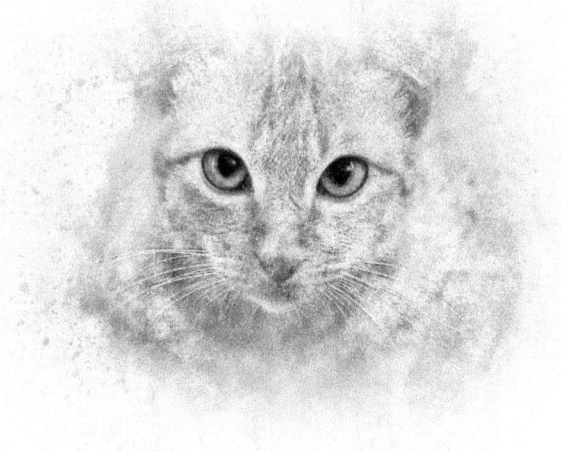

This Is My Dream

This is my dream.
You and me
In this magical forest
Your arms wrapped lovingly around me
Your thoughts filled with nothing but me
No one to tell me to wake up
No one to tell me to give up
Cause I have you here
I will keep you here
In this magical forest
You and me
This is my dream

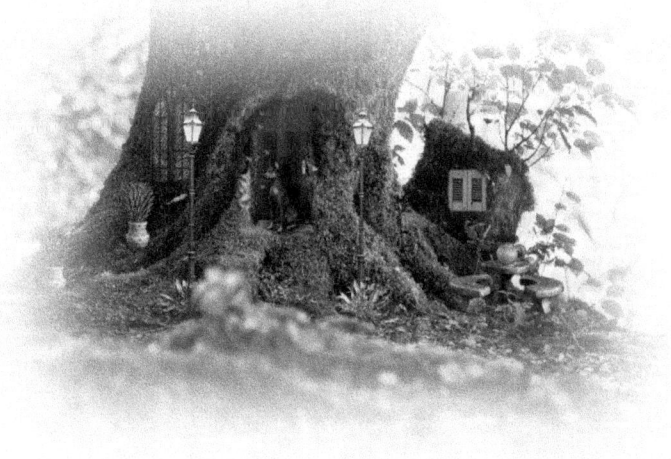

ALICE

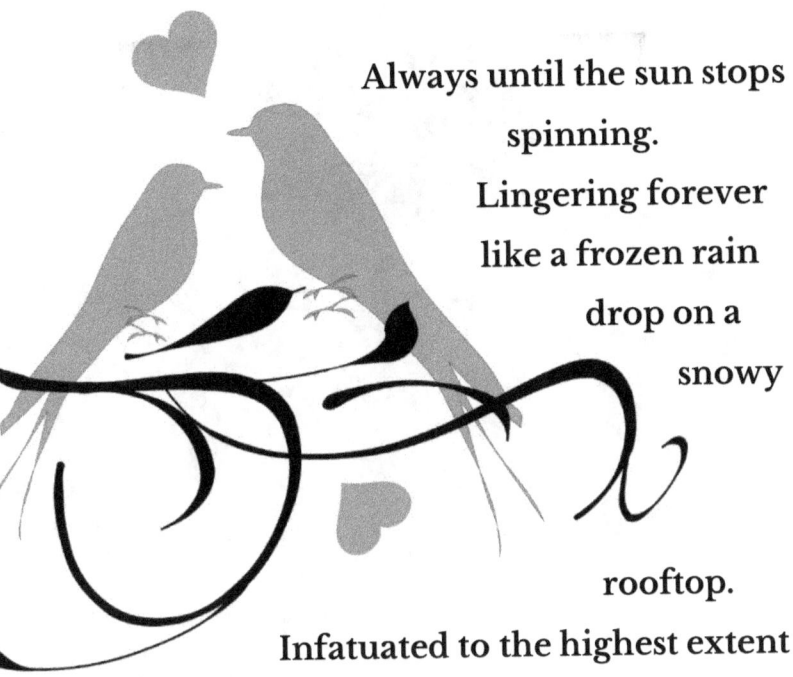

Always until the sun stops spinning.
Lingering forever like a frozen rain drop on a snowy rooftop.
Infatuated to the highest extent but it is not fleeting.
Caring with the ferocity of a mother lion.
Protective.
Entrance like a pair of bees drawn to each other and moving by instinct. Enthralled by a force. Ready to follow each other through the sky eternally.

H.S.W.

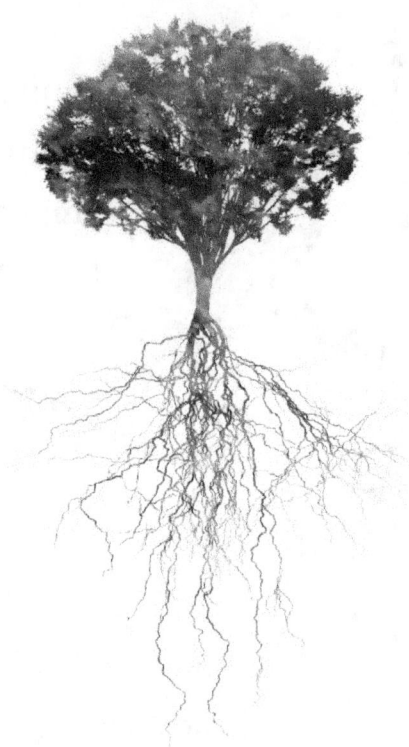

I think I froze the first time I saw you
You strode across the asphalt with your hands
at your heart and your tapioca pearl eyes wide.

I think I gasped the first time I heard you sing.
You belted that high note with ease.
I knew then that you had me.

I think I screamed too much the first time you ranked high.
I was so happy for you. I wanted you to reach the sky.

I know I cried when they announced your name.
I knew it was both an end and a beginning.

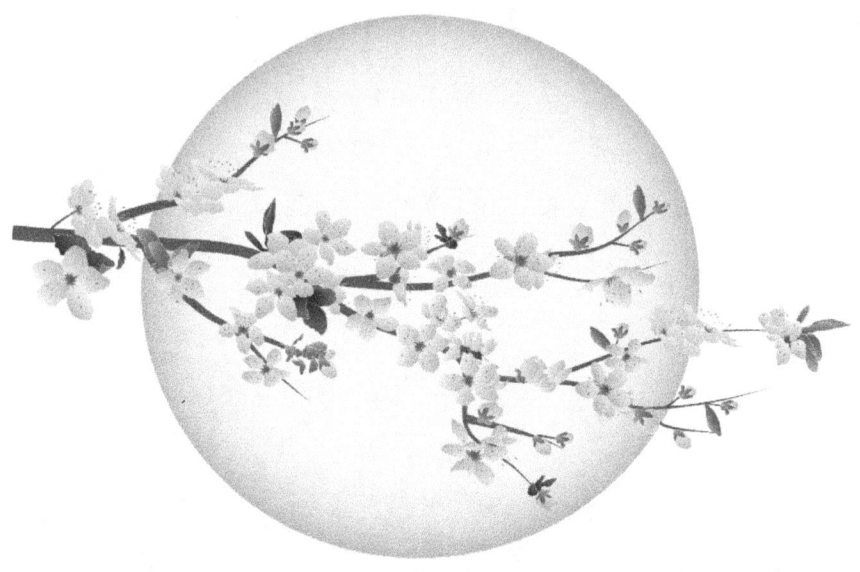

I knew I would love you forever. My love for you will burn bright like a flame, a flame that will not go out, not ever.

The boy with the Moon

My muse
The reason I write
The reason I sing
The reason I fight
The reason I dream

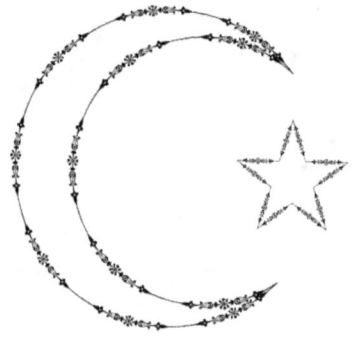

The Boy with Puppy Eyes

Smile at me
And I melt
Look at me
And I blush
Sing for me
And I listen
Sweat for me
And I scream and shout
Weep for me
And I will weep for you
Be with me
And I will always be with you.

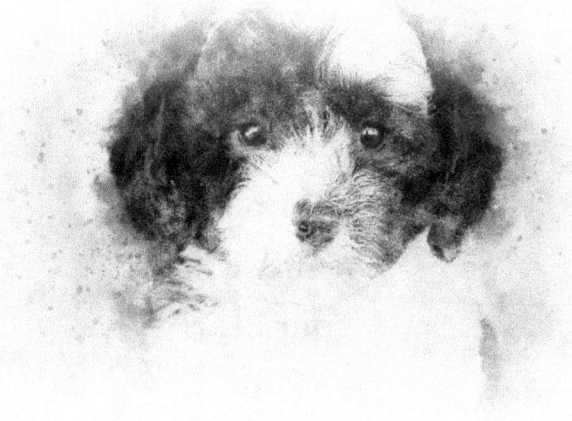

The Boy With the Heart Smile

Your voice

Gravely

Husky

Your hair

Silky

Thick

Your face

Dimpled

Creamy white

Your heart

Pure

Open

Warm

Strawberry Boy

Words that come to mind when I think of you;
Wild
Loud
Odd
Funny
Silly
I am never bored when I watch you.
Loyal
Loving
Affectionate
Passionate
I always know I am in your thoughts.

TO MY SOFT ANGEL

My Mirror
Your pain is known to me.
It is mirrored in my heart
Your faith is real to me.
Your God is my God.
Your scars are visible to me.
I have been hurt too.
Your heart is known to me.
I have been lonely too.
My love reaches out to you,
To heal you, to heal me.

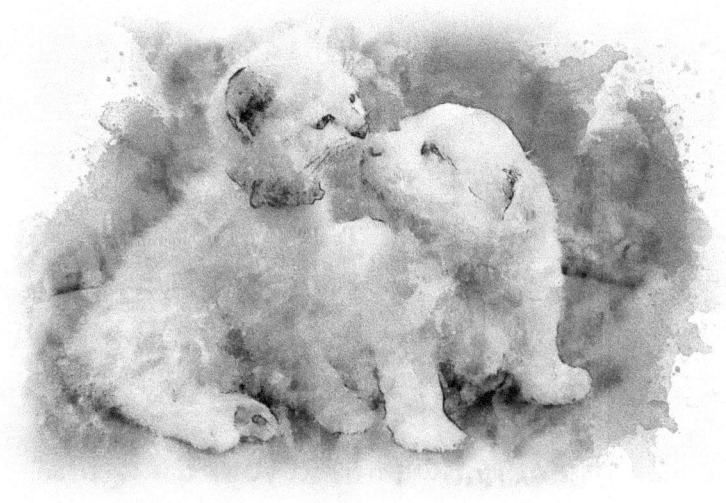

The Boy with the Dimples

This dimple on your cheek
Is there to me weak.
The sound of your voice
Is not a simple noise.
It is the voice of a songbird
Of one I have never heard
Cause your voice is only yours
A voice I cannot ignore
When you talk, I listen
When you sing, I soften
This freckle on your neck.
Is not a simple speck
It marks you as unique
Like the dimples on your cheeks.

THE WHITE RABBIT

When you smile,
The corners of
my mouth lift,
And my cheeks
from round apples.
When you laugh,
A tiny 'aww' escapes
my lips
When you sing,
My ears perk
up
I listen
intently,
Not wanting to miss a note
When you dance,
My heart pounds in my chest,
And I can hardly catch my breath.

"The adventure isn't over yet. The Key to Wonderland is your love Alice.
　Let it never rust
　　May you never lose it."

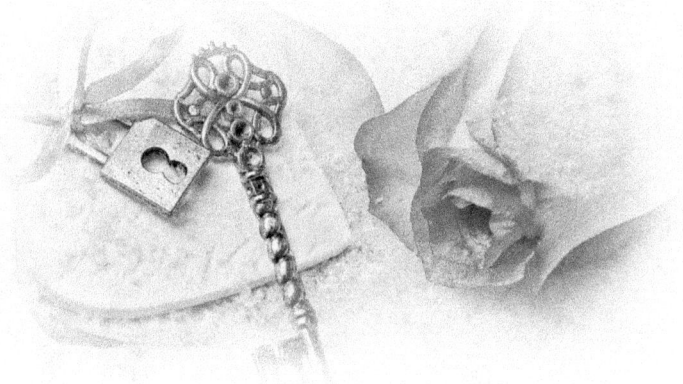

The next adventure...is waiting for you.
Open the door...

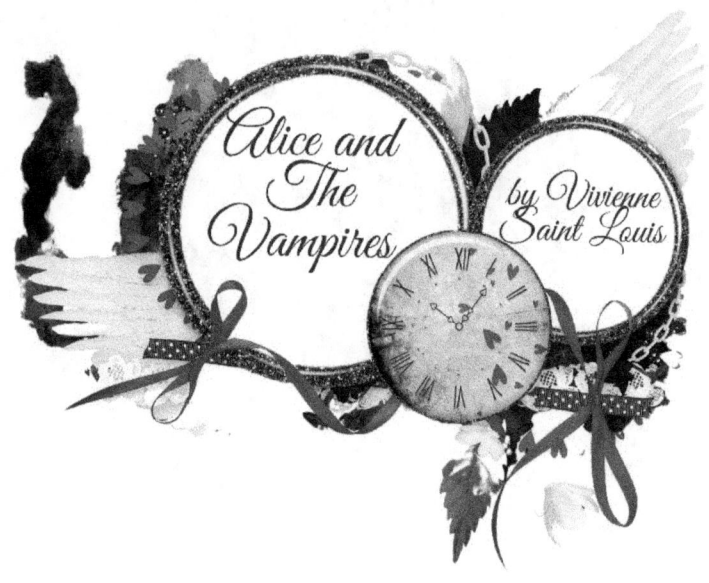

Coming soon

Also By

If you enjoyed this book, check out these other titles Vivienne Saint Louis

Check out Vivienne's other Poetry Collection

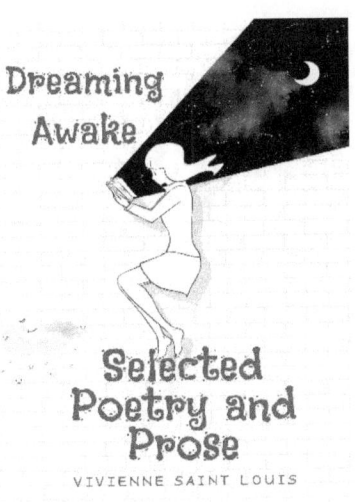

The Sisters Affinity Series

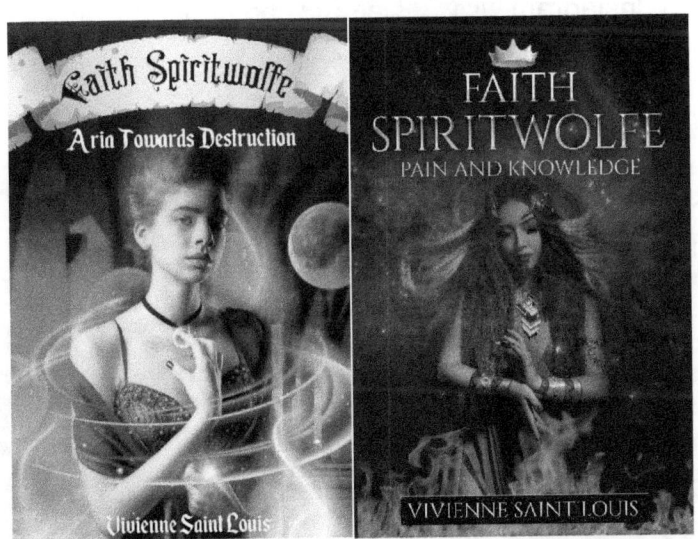

Find Vivienne on social media!

Twitter www.twitter.com/vivi-saint
Instagram www.instagram.com/viviennesaint
Website https://vivisaint.weebly.com/

About the Author

Vivienne Saint Louis is a writer, lyricist, and a teacher. She has been writing and collecting her work since she was 13 years old.

Now she lives in Japan where she teaches English as a Second Language.

Vivienne enjoys playing tennis, figure skating, dancing, K-Pop, and video games.

www.ingramcontent.com/pod-product-compliance
Lightning Source LLC
Chambersburg PA
CBHW070838220526
45466CB00002B/821